# RESET

## BY NICK HALL

**#JesusChangesEverything**

**OUTREACH**®

RESET
© 2016 by Outreach, Inc.

Published by Outreach, Inc., Colorado Springs, CO 80919
www.Outreach.com

ISBN: 9781942027478
Cover Design by Tim Downs
Interior Design by Alexia Garaventa
Written by Nick Hall
Edited by Tia Smith

Printed in the United States of America

A dozen years ago, I was a college student in North Dakota, surrounded by good friends, a decent social scene, and classes that for the most part I enjoyed. Even so, a single question plagued my thoughts, coming around way too often—unannounced, unwelcomed, and unkind. I would soon learn that most of my buddies were asking the very same question, and that, just like me, they hadn't landed on an answer yet. The question: "Is this all there is?"

Five straightforward, seemingly innocent words, and yet, man, did they wreak havoc in my life.

The problem for my friends and me was that we were generally well-behaved, churchgoing guys. We did our best to show up on Sundays for church and would even occasionally make a midweek prayer service or Bible study. We went to the events, prayed the prayers, and sang the songs. And yet something wasn't adding up.

The stories we were learning about in Scripture—of people taking huge risks, engaging in exciting adventures, and compelling others to lay it all down for the sake of Jesus—looked nothing like the lives we were living. The boldest thing you could say about my friends and me most weeks was that we successfully avoided the parties and maintained "good guy" status … not exactly Book of Acts kind of stuff!

There had to be more to life than trying our best not to do bad things. We *knew* there had to be more. We just weren't entirely sure where to find it.

My friends and I knew deep down that there was promise and potential to be found at the local church, even as we acknowledged that for most of our peers, the concept of "church" was loaded with emotional baggage and wounds from the past. Personally, I grew up in a situation where my dad's side was Catholic, my mom's side was Presbyterian,

MY COLLEGE BUDDIES
AND I KNEW THERE
HAD TO BE MORE
TO LIFE THAN TRYING
OUR BEST
NOT TO DO BAD THINGS.
WE JUST WEREN'T
ENTIRELY SURE
WHERE TO FIND IT.

my family went to an evangelical church, I was part of a Baptist youth group, and I attended a Lutheran high school. Needless to say, there was a lot of confusion for me surrounding what "church" even meant … and more than a few barriers to overcome. (Why all the division? Couldn't we all just get along?)

## Taking Our PULSE

My buddies and I looked inside the church and saw disunity, hypocrisy, and way too many people bored out of their minds, and we looked outside the church and saw despair that was leading to self-harm, substance abuse, and suicide. Something had to give.

Not knowing what else to do, someone had the idea that we should start praying. So, a few of us began meeting each week to pray for wisdom and change on our campus. It was obvious what the problems were; what wasn't so obvious—to us, anyway—was exactly how they were going to get solved. Around that same time, one of my professors assigned a project to my English class. It was a fifteen-page business proposal and fifteen-minute presentation on some product or service we thought could impact the campus. This was supposed to be a group project, but as soon as she issued the parameters, I knew I needed to go solo. What I intended to present was the need for a "Jesus movement," right there at North Dakota State University, and I figured nobody else in my class would want to risk their grade like that. I'd had a phrase—a mission, if you will—banging around in my brain for some time: *My life exists to put Christ at the pulse of a generation.*

I knew that's what God was calling me to do, but the fine print of that calling wouldn't become legible until much, much later.

I got clearance from my professor to do the project on my own, rushed home and sat in front of

WE LOOKED
INSIDE THE CHURCH
AND SAW DISUNITY,
AND WE LOOKED
OUTSIDE THE CHURCH
AND SAW DESPAIR.
SOMETHING
HAD TO GIVE.

my laptop with my fingers over the keyboard, and ... *nothing*. Not only did I have no clue how to write a business proposal, but I also had no idea how to bring my campus to Christ. "God," my prayer that afternoon went, "help!"

In the end, in keeping with my life's mission, I wound up titling my proposal "PULSE." In it, I explained the devastating trends taking hold of our campus—the drinking, the drugging, the soaring suicide rate, the whole deal—and then explained, in the most straightforward terms I could think of, Jesus's invitation for us to start again. After I delivered my presentation to the class, I took my proposal to the campus copy shop and made a stack of copies that I handed out to friends of mine who led campus ministries for the three big schools in our area. I told them that God had laid this vision on my heart and that I was interested in their feedback. "Please read this," I asked them. "Pray about it, and then let's talk."

I'D HAD A PHRASE
BANGING AROUND
IN MY BRAIN
FOR SOME TIME:
*MY LIFE EXISTS TO
PUT CHRIST
AT THE PULSE
OF A GENERATION.*
I KNEW THAT'S WHAT
GOD WAS CALLING ME
TO DO.

Astoundingly, they *did* read it. They did pray about it. And we did talk. What's more, they wanted in on what we collectively believed God was up to. Those guys offered to help out, and soon thereafter, *their* friends, and their *friends*' friends joined in. Before I knew it, a ragtag team of college guys and girls had flanked me, all of whom were ready to serve however they could. One of them fixed my sorry graphics. Another tightened up the flow from an editorial standpoint. Another gave me ideas for how to market a campaign like PULSE.

There were people who were good at fundraising, and people who were good at networking, and people who were good at PR, and within a month of that English class presentation, the PULSE train had left the station and was screaming down the tracks. I didn't get much rest during that season, but who cared about sleep? God was on the move.

In order to reach the numbers we hoped with the life-changing message of Jesus, we decided the best tack we could take was to host a series of events culminating with a massive outreach. Most of the students in our community weren't involved in a local church or a campus ministry, and even those who were plugged in—roughly one thousand of the twenty-two thousand there—were statistically unlikely to "share their faith." (According to most studies, less than 15 percent of Christians of any age regularly tell others about Jesus.)[1] If we were going to reach our campuses, the math problem wasn't going to get solved by simple addition; we needed multiplication.

We approached those who were engaged in campus ministry and asked them to lead a prayer group, and then we started telling everyone we could about those groups. If someone wasn't involved in a prayer group because the times didn't work for them, we

1 LifeWay produced one such study recently: http://www.lifeway.com/Article/research-survey-sharing-christ-2012.

asked what time *did* work for them and then launched a new group on the spot. In short order, we had rolled out more than twenty prayer groups that met every morning and every evening of the week and some afternoons.

Next, we asked students to give up coffee and shopping and going out on dates in favor of donating funds to our cause, and to everyone's surprise, we raised more than $30,000 in a three-month span of time. That money went toward renting a facility and covering production costs for our first event, held in the spring of 2006. Five thousand students packed the venue, one thousand of whom surrendered their lives to Jesus. The following year, the movement spread to ten thousand students, and the year after that, North Dakota's governor and first lady came out and opened one of our events and thousands more met Jesus. We were floored. God was putting his Son at the pulse of our generation, right in our midst.

REACHING
THAT MANY KIDS
WITH THE LIFE-CHANGING
MESSAGE OF JESUS
WAS A MATH PROBLEM
THAT WASN'T GOING
TO GET SOLVED
BY SIMPLE ADDITION.
MULTIPLICATION
WAS THE ONLY WAY.

# Growth and More Growth

By 2009, more than fifty thousand students had been impacted, and more than ten thousand of them had responded to the Gospel message, making PULSE one of the largest student-led evangelism movements in American history. By that time, we had filed paperwork to become an official nonprofit, and that fall, the three of us who made up our staff opened our "global headquarters" in Minneapolis, Minnesota. With the eagerness of a playful puppy, we asked God what was next.

As it turns out, "what was next" would involve *a lot* of students learning about grace, about forgiveness, about the reset that is available in Christ. To date, our team has taken that message to three million students and to every state in the Union. *Together 2016*, our nationwide event on the National Mall in Washington, DC, has set its aim to rally more than one million people—all gathered at the same time under the same name: Jesus. And to shoot completely straight with you? I think we're just getting started. People's needs are that deep, and the reset that Jesus offers is that real.

One of the greatest joys of the last few years has been seeing local churches line up to help. Churches are collections of messy, imperfect people who carry out Jesus's mission in a messy and imperfect way, and by the dozens, church leaders reached out to us to say, "We want the do-over you're talking about. We want it for our people individually, and we want it for our entire body, for our *church*."

They wanted to strip back all the layers they'd added to Jesus and re-encounter *him*, simply for who he is. They wanted to get back to prayer. To the words of Jesus. To faith-based living. To community service. To being known for *loving* well instead

BY 2009, MORE THAN
FIFTY THOUSAND
STUDENTS HAD BEEN
IMPACTED, AND MORE
THAN TEN THOUSAND
OF THEM HAD
RESPONDED TO THE
GOSPEL MESSAGE,
MAKING PULSE ONE
OF THE LARGEST
STUDENT-LED
EVANGELISM MOVEMENTS
IN AMERICAN HISTORY.

of for *judging* well. And so the *Reset* churchwide experience was born. In fact, the reason you are holding this book is that a church nearby is about to spend an entire month exploring what a spiritual reset might involve for them, and they want *you* to be involved.

## The Resets We Require

Over the past decade, at events from Fargo to Fresno, from Jacksonville to Jersey City, from the Deep South to the Midwest, from the West Coast to the East Coast, and in every major city in between, I have met people who are (quite literally) dying for a second chance. A fresh start. A reset. They are dog-tired from pretending they have it all together, they are disillusioned by their letdown of a life, and they are desperate for a solution that works. They need a do-over in their marriage. Or in their finances. Or in their relationships with their

THE REASON YOU
ARE HOLDING THIS BOOK
IS THAT A CHURCH
NEARBY IS ABOUT
TO SPEND
AN ENTIRE MONTH
EXPLORING WHAT A
SPIRITUAL RESET
INVOLVES,
AND THEY WANT YOU
TO BE INVOLVED.

friends. They need a do-over at work, at school, at home, or in their thought life. Their habits are distracting them. Their priorities are paralyzing them. Their self-talk is beating them down. And by the time they are standing there in front of me, they've reached what is now a very frayed end of their rope.

"It's my abusive father," they'll say.

"It's the cocaine."

"It's food."

"I've been stealing from work."

"I can't quit cutting."

"I spend more time playing video games than interacting with living, breathing human beings."

"I thought I could kick my porn habit, but I can't."

"My life is a joke."

"Nobody cares."

"I hate myself."

"I've been cheating on my wife."

"I'm broke."

"I'm depressed."

"I never say the right thing."

"I'm addicted to pills."

"I don't want to live."

In these and a thousand other ways, they are asking the very same question of life that I asked when I was a college freshman: *Is this all there is?*

Over the years, my colleagues at PULSE and I have made a habit of collecting this type of input from the guys and girls who come to our events. Sometimes we receive input from firsthand conversations. Sometimes that input is texted in. Sometimes people send us e-mails after the fact. But regardless of how we receive it, along the way we've noticed that it always fits within one of four broad categories. People want Jesus to reset their *heart*, their *mind*, their *voice*, or their *hands*. They want a do-over in terms of their faith, which is an issue of the heart; or in terms of their thought life, which is an issue of the mind; or in terms of the words they speak, which is an issue of the voice; or in terms of how they invest their time, money, and energies, which we refer to as an issue of the hands. And so when it came time to put together a churchwide experience, we knew we wanted those four topics front and center.

If you choose to engage with a local church in the *Reset* experience, and I hope that you will, you'll notice that each week's topic is a one-line prayer that addresses one of those themes:

Week 1: "Jesus, Reset My Heart"

Week 2: "Jesus, Reset My Mind"

Week 3: "Jesus, Reset My Voice"

Week 4: "Jesus, Reset My Hands"

I'd like to contextualize those categories, one at a time. First up, let's talk about the heart.

# Reset 1: "Jesus, Reset My Heart"

When my siblings and I were kids, my parents had a cabin on a lake in Minnesota where we used to vacation every year. That little house provided us countless incredible memories, including one of my all-time favorites: *bats*. For several years, my dad declared all-out war on a posse of bats that planned its family reunions in our cabin, and generally speaking, he lost every battle he fought. That is, until he called The Batman.

The Batman was a bat specialist living in Frazee, Minnesota, who was renowned for his amazing ability to rid a place of bats. I'll admit I was a little let down when he pulled up in a beat-up pickup instead of the Batmobile, but what he lacked in style he made up for in substance. It was The Batman who taught my family that bats can squeeze into a hole the size of a quarter; that bats and humans were never meant to cohabitate and thus posed a real threat to our health as long as they were in our house; and that regardless of how many bats my dad took down or shooed away, there would be more bats there the next night. "I want them *gone*," my dad said in a grave tone to The Batman, and so The Batman went to work. He located the tiniest nooks and crannies that my dad had completely overlooked, he stuffed them full with some sort of special bat-repelling caulk, and he proudly produced an invoice that my dad was all too happy to pay. And from that day forward, those bats needed a new hideout.

As I've thought about it, I believe our hearts work in the same way. We know we're vulnerable to attack from forces that don't want us to thrive in life, and so we go after the big holes, plugging them with anything we can find—habits, distractions, addictions, and the like. And yet we find ourselves still at war. Our situation grows more and more hopeless until we allow a specialist to come in. In this case, that specialist is Jesus, the One who knows where the overlooked crevices are. He plugs every last hole, he secures the perimeter of our souls, and he says, "In me, you'll be safe from attack."

Whenever I talk to students after PULSE events, I tell them the very same thing: "You already knew that a life free from infestation was possible. You just didn't know where to find it. I'm telling you where to find it now: It's found in Jesus, alone." That longing in our hearts for more? In Jesus, that longing is satisfied. We can live life perfectly content—at peace, at ease, at last. What's more, we don't have to earn this fulfillment; it has been paid in full by Jesus, the One who died so that we can live.

If you're like me, you have spent most of your life working to fill your holes with acceptance, accolades, awards, trophies, grades, money, recognition, independence, the works. We're so accustomed to striving for achievement that the offer of *freedom that's actually free* is something we hardly can compute. And yet that's exactly what we're dealing with here. Ephesians 2:8–10 puts it this way:

> *God saved you by his grace when you believed. And you can't take credit for this; it is a gift from God. Salvation is not a reward for the good things we have done, so none of us can boast about it. For we are God's masterpiece. He has created us anew in Christ Jesus, so we can do the good things he planned for us long ago.* (NLT)

The message of a heart reset isn't about fixing yourself, getting it together, or getting it right so that you can make yourself "good enough" for a holy God. It's about allowing a holy God to completely

JESUS PLUGS EVERY
LAST HOLE, HE SECURES
THE PERIMETER
OF OUR SOULS,
AND HE SAYS,
"IN ME, YOU'LL BE SAFE
FROM ATTACK.

take over so that his togetherness, his rightness, can flow through you. That's all "righteousness" is—God's "rightness," and our "rightness" in him. And Scripture says that right living always begins in the heart. "Guard your heart above all else," Proverbs 4:23 says, "for it determines the course of your life" (NLT). "Wherever your treasure is, there the desires of your heart will also be," says Matthew 6:21 (NLT). "A good person produces good things from the treasury of a good heart," Matthew 12:35 affirms, "and an evil person produces evil things from the treasury of an evil heart" (NLT). When a heart changes for good, a life changes for good—and so we begin with the heart. We begin with faith. We begin with allowing Jesus to reset us from the inside out. A heart reset begins when we stop putting our hope in what we need to do and turn that hope to what Jesus has already done for us.

## Reset 2: "Jesus, Reset My Mind"

Once our heart (faith) has been reset in Jesus, the sky is the limit on the level of health and wholeness we can experience, and one of the first places that transformation shows up is in the patterns of thought we entertain.

Is it just me, or do our moms get smarter the older we get? Now that I'm a grown man, I am finding that all those things my mom used to say—her Greatest Hits of cautions, considerations, and critiques—are actually (and astoundingly!) true. One of her Mom-isms was this: "You are what you think about." And you know what? It's 100 percent true.

With this in mind, it's no wonder so many of us are depressed, demoralized, defeated, and distraught. Just look at the thoughts we let in! Stressful thoughts. Impure thoughts. Negative thoughts. Thoughts of impending doom. How many of *your* thoughts on a given day are helping versus hurting your cause?

To complicate matters, fixing our perilous thought patterns isn't as straightforward as just "deciding to think something else." Sure, we can contrive happier thoughts for a moment, an hour, or perhaps even a day, but according to the truths of Scripture, eventually what's *really* in our heart is going to totally flood our unsuspecting mind. And when the heart is corrupted, our thoughts wind up being jaded, sarcastic, ungrateful, unhelpful, despairing, and unkind. Again, we're back to the heart. When the heart is reset, the mind can be reset. "I'm *not* hopeless," we can finally think. "I'm *not* worthless. I'm *not* uncared for, unloved, or unseen. I have a heavenly Father who has adopted me, and I'm destined for amazing things by his will."

When we allow Jesus to reset us, heart and mind, we begin to fight not *for* victory but *from* it—we fight from the place of knowing that, in Jesus, the victory has already been won. At last, confidence and hope are ours.

Think of it this way: If a kid grows up in an abusive home, is told every day that he is a loser, is denied basic provisions such as food and clothing, and is literally turned out onto the street and locked out of his home whenever his mom is in one of her "moods," his chances of success in life later on are all but shot. But take a kid who lives in a nurturing environment where healthy boundaries are set, Mom and Dad express love and admiration for their son freely, and all of his needs are met, and far more times than not, that kid is going to thrive. He still may face tough challenges and circumstances in life, but that firm foundation of respect and love will equip him to prevail.

God is our nurturing Father, and we are that beloved child. Despite the difficulties we are sure to face in life, to the extent we continue to walk with him, we will continue to prevail. This is what the apostle Paul is talking about when he says, "Do not conform to the pattern of this world, but be transformed by the renewing of your mind" (Romans 12:2, NIV).

WHEN WE ALLOW JESUS
TO RESET US,
HEART AND MIND,
WE BEGIN TO FIGHT
NOT *FOR* VICTORY
BUT *FROM* IT.
AT LAST,
CONFIDENCE AND HOPE
ARE OURS.

# Reset 3: "Jesus, Reset My Voice"

Along the same lines, when we allow Jesus to reset our heart, in addition to our thoughts being transformed, our words get an extreme makeover too. What we say has the power to birth life or to quicken death in the people we say it to, according to the themes of the Bible (see Proverbs 18:21, specifically). So this shift from speaking negative, gossipy, cynical, angry, self-interested, and vile words to speaking words filled with gentleness, kindness, gratitude, optimism, love, and hope is a consequential one to say the least.

I've seen this reset of the voice unfold in hundreds of people's lives, and it's a shocker every time. The young woman who used to be right at the center of all the office gossip now catches herself and actually stands up for the absent person. The guy who always laughed at the crude locker room jokes now finds a way to make his exit before the

WHAT WE SAY
HAS THE POWER TO
BIRTH LIFE
OR TO
QUICKEN DEATH
IN THE PEOPLE
WE SAY IT TO.

punch line hits. The daughter who made a sport out of complaining now stops herself midsentence and finds something to be thankful for.

The dad who came on strong every time his son brought home his schoolwork finds himself softening: "I can see from the look on your face that you're proud of this grade," he hears himself say. "Tell me about it ..."

The wife, realizing her husband forgot to pick up chicken broth for her soup on the way home, refuses to get frustrated, choosing instead to smile and say, "I understand. Some days, I would forget my head if it weren't attached."

The sales associate whose colleague gets the promotion instead of him refuses to gripe about the injustice of it all, choosing instead to congratulate her and ask if there is anything he can do to help her thrive.

The couple, in response to their neighbor who "helpfully" points out that their front yard is looking unkempt, refuses to get snarky, choosing instead to acknowledge how well-manicured the neighbor's lawn always is.

The hurried, harried mom who is being held up by a painfully slow grocery store checkout clerk refuses to get huffy, choosing instead to exhale her annoyance, thank him for his efforts, and help him bag her groceries.

The driver who gets cut off in traffic refuses to erupt, choosing instead to say, "Wow. They must be in a real hurry. Hope they get where they're going in one piece …"

That person you know who always seems to be upbeat and positive? Once your voice is reset in Jesus, incredibly, *fantastically*, it's you.

When I first started PULSE, a local pastor in Fargo called and told me he had heard about the ministry and wondered if there was any way he could support the work my friends and I were doing. He'd started a ministry years prior and knew the challenges we would face; he wanted to save me from falling into some of the same traps he had landed in, which was an offer I couldn't turn down. I had been asking God to send a mentor my way, and this turn of events felt like divine intervention all the way around.

Mike Montgomery not only became an invaluable mentor to me but also a beloved friend. His contributions to my life are way too many to count, but there is a theme underlying them all, and it centers on *wisdom with words*. The interactions I've had with Mike—by now a thousand? more?—have consistently been characterized by positivity, encouragement, laughter, gratitude, and joy. I can honestly say that following every conversation with Mike, I am a better Christ follower, a better husband, a better dad, a better leader, and a better friend.

I CAN HONESTLY SAY
THAT FOLLOWING
EVERY CONVERSATION
WITH MIKE,
I AM A BETTER
CHRIST FOLLOWER,
A BETTER HUSBAND,
A BETTER DAD,
A BETTER LEADER,
AND
A BETTER FRIEND.

Case in point: Just two weeks ago, I was stressed out and feeling anxious while in Nashville for some meetings. It was ten o'clock at night when I finally decided I needed to phone Mike. I halfway hoped he wouldn't pick up—I didn't want to interrupt his family time or freak him out, given the late hour. But when he did pick up and I heard his calming voice, I breathed a sigh of relief. "Hey, Nick!" he said in his enthusiastic way. "How's it going? I've been praying for you!"

Mike and I caught up for the first few minutes of the call, but then there was that long pause that told him there was a deeper reason I'd reached out. I told Mike that I felt like I'd been pushing lately, that I'd been running so hard that I felt worn out physically, emotionally—even spiritually. The word that kept coming to mind as I talked with Mike was "striving." In our efforts to plan for the gathering on the National Mall, I'd been relentless in my pursuit of more meetings, more partnerships, more sys-tems created to follow up with those who would surrender their lives to Jesus, and on and on it went. In short, I was falling into the trap of believing it all rested on my shoulders. I knew that striving wasn't something God encouraged in the Bible, and I knew that if I did not get this spirit of striving subdued in me, it would eat me alive.

Mike wasted no time on the heels of my expla-nation. "Let me pray for you," he said and then did. "Listen, if you don't last, Nick, this whole thing—God's call on your life, the mission he has you on, all your hard work up to this point—it's all for nothing. I'd like to work with you on revising your schedule so that you feel at peace with your days and weeks instead of feeling enslaved to them."

We talked for a few minutes more, and then Mike suggested that I clear my calendar for two days upon returning home from the road and take my wife, Tiffany, on a mini vacation. He knew that I was feeling adrift at sea and that reconnecting with what is most important to me—Tiffany tops that list, second only to Jesus—would be the quickest way to reanchor my soul. I flew home the next day, repacked a bag, and took Tiffany to a cabin in northern Minnesota. Mike was right: The time away rebuilt something that had been torn down in my inner person.

We all need a friend like Mike.[2] We can all *be* a friend like Mike when Jesus is allowed to reset our mouth. James 3 says that wisdom "begins with a holy life and is characterized by getting along with others" (verse 17, MSG). Isn't that a simple and yet profound statement? Holiness comes down to getting along with others? *Seriously?*

Jesus is totally serious about this stuff. Under the inspiration of the Holy Spirit, James goes on:

2 I also tell this story in *Reset: Jesus Changes Everything* (Colorado Springs, CO: Multnomah, 2016).

*It [he's still speaking of a "holy life" here] is gentle and reasonable, overflowing with mercy and blessings, not hot one day and cold the next, not two-faced. You can develop a healthy, robust community that lives right with God and enjoy its results only if you do the hard work of getting along with each other, treating each other with dignity and honor. (verse 18, MSG)*

When our faith gets reset, our thoughts get reset. And when our thoughts get reset, the words we speak get wonderfully reset too. Mark my words here: You soften your heart toward Jesus, and *everything's* about to change. Your self-talk. Your speech. Even your investments of energy and time. Let's look at that fourth reset now.

# Reset 4: "Jesus, Reset My Hands"

There's a terrific story in Scripture about the weighty, divine opportunities that get placed in a pair of reset hands. Spend a few minutes reading Acts 8:26–40 the next time you have a Bible or Bible app in front of you. The gist of the story is this: One day, one of Jesus's disciples, Philip, was having a conversation with God (this is all that prayer is, really) when he was given a prompting to head across town to a deserted place, for reasons that would be explained later on. Now, I don't know what you would say in response, but I'd be a little hesitant. *Go to the bad part of town? By myself? Now? God, is that really you?*

Philip wasted no time going. The passage says exactly that: "He got up and went" (verse 27, MSG).

When Philip arrived at that deserted road across town, he happened upon an African man—a royal official, he would soon discover—who was making his way from Ethiopia to Jerusalem. While he rode along in his chariot, he was reading the Bible, from the Old Testament book of Isaiah.

As Philip took in this scene—the sense of expectancy, the deserted road, the man in the chariot racing by—he received a second whisper: "Climb into the chariot" (verse 29, MSG). Had I been Philip, I'd have protested. *Seriously, God? Run alongside this guy's ride and just heave myself onto the seat?*

Philip wasted no time and immediately started running. The passage says exactly that, too: "Running up alongside, Philip heard the eunuch reading Isaiah and asked, 'Do you understand what you're reading?'" (verse 30, MSG).

The royal official said he had no clue what he was reading—could Philip help him out?

And so it was, that as the chariot continued racing up the deserted road, Philip heaved himself onto the chariot's seat and explained to the man the mysteries of salvation and baptism and living in lock-step with Jesus. About this time, the chariot happened by a stream of water, upon which the eunuch said, "Hey. There's some water. Why can't I trust Jesus and get baptized here and now?"

Moments later, the chariot had been pulled to a stop, the men had disembarked, and one was baptizing the other as God in heaven surely smiled.

The reason I love this story is that it so perfectly encapsulates what someone with reset hands longs to do: to know Jesus better, and to act more like him.

When your hands get reset by Jesus, you develop an insatiable appetite for accepting, forgiving, loving, enjoying, serving, helping, and persevering with the people he died to save. And you know that the way to live out such radical acceptance and love is by communing with the living God. You *want* to pray, because when you talk to God, you are reminded of people he wants you to invest in. You

I LOVE THIS STORY
BECAUSE IT
ENCAPSULATES
WHAT SOMEONE WITH
RESET HANDS
LONGS TO DO:
TO KNOW JESUS BETTER,
AND TO ACT MORE
LIKE HIM.

*want* to read, because when you expose yourself to books about God, you learn how to live the life that will truly satisfy. You *want* to go to church, because when you hear your pastor talk, you discover principles that will make you a kinder, more generous version of yourself. You want to do anything you can do to know Jesus better, because it's in knowing him that you become like him. Some people may "do good" simply to be known as a do-gooder. But those who have been reset in Jesus do good because they have encountered a good God. God has captured their heart, their mind, their voice, and their full attention, and now when he says, "Go," *they waste no time going there.*

Hebrews 11 is referred to as the Hall of Faith because it honors those who walked by faith instead of sight, who allowed their heart reset to totally alter how they spent their days. There, we read of Noah, who was warned about a rainstorm of gigantic proportions and thus built an ark, *just as God had asked*.

We read of Abraham, who was called to go to an undisclosed place and live as a stranger in a foreign land. He went, *just as God had asked*.

We read of Isaac and Jacob, who joined their father and grandfather, Abraham, living as tent-camping nomads, *just as God had asked*.

We read of Sarah, who decided to believe God when he told her that despite her senior-citizen status, she was about to bear a child and thus begin a line of descendants "as numerous as the stars in the sky" (verse 12, NIV), *just as God had asked*.

We read of Moses's parents, who hid the child from the Egyptian authorities actively working to kill all Hebrew babies, *just as God had asked*. And later, of Moses himself, who led the Israelite people through the Red Sea and toward the Promised Land, *just as God had asked*.

We read of Rahab, a prostitute living in Jericho who hid the Israeli spies scouting out the land they'd been promised, *just as God had asked*.

The litany concludes with these staggering words:

> *And what more shall I say? I [the writer*
> *of Hebrews] do not have time to tell*
> *about Gideon, Barak, Samson and*
> *Jephthah, about David and Samuel and*
> *the prophets, who through faith con-*
> *quered kingdoms, administered justice,*
> *and gained what was promised; who*
> *shut the mouths of lions, quenched the*
> *fury of the flames, and escaped the*
> *edge of the sword; whose weakness was*
> *turned to strength; and who became*
> *powerful in battle and routed foreign*

*armies. Women received back their dead, raised to life again. There were others who were tortured, refusing to be released so that they might gain an even better resurrection. Some faced jeers and flogging, and even chains and imprisonment. They were put to death by stoning; they were sawed in two; they were killed by the sword. They went about in sheepskins and goatskins, destitute, persecuted and mistreated— the world was not worthy of them. They wandered in deserts and mountains, living in caves and in holes in the ground. (verses 32–38, NIV)*

These verses showcase the lengths that re-set individuals are willing to go in order to do what God has asked them to do, and I have to tell you, their faith is instructive to me. They didn't have passive faith, faith that loves to talk a good game but shies away when the stakes are high. No, they possessed active faith, faith with works, as James 2:17 exhorts us to have. Because their faith had been reset, their thoughts had been reset. And because their thoughts had been reset, their words had been reset. And because what they believed, what they thought about, and what they talked about had been utterly transformed, *the things they chose to do* looked different. They eagerly spent time getting to know God. And then when God said *go*, they went. When he said *serve*, they served. When he said *conquer*, they conquered. When he said *seek justice*, they sought justice. And in the end, because of their *amazing, activated faith*, the "world was not worthy of them" (Hebrews 11:38, NIV).

I want to be like that. I want to be remembered as someone who lived for Jesus. And given you've stuck with me throughout these pages thus far, something tells me you do too.

## The Thing I Bet You'd Regret

Since the early days of PULSE, each time I have seen yet another guy or girl choose to surrender leadership of their life to Jesus, a specific image has popped into my mind, that of a person adrift at sea being lifted from those waters onto a rescue boat. I was handed fresh appreciation for just how powerful turbulent waters can be earlier this year when I was in Florida for a meeting and some businessmen I was with said they wanted to take me deep-sea fishing. Normally I would have declined, but they said they'd pay. (Score!) Plus, I've always loved fishing and didn't want to pass up what might be a once-in-a-lifetime experience. I said yes. By that evening, it was a yes I'd totally regret.

We departed West Palm Beach by boat that afternoon, and within thirty minutes, I felt sick. The boat was pitching so terribly that I looked around for life preservers, just in case. "This is not fishing," I kept thinking. "This is *bouncing*. Plus, I'm cold."

As the waves rocked us back and forth, we tried to make the best of it. "Train your eyes on the horizon," our driver shouted above the waves and wind, "and the seasickness will be subdued." I did what he said, picking out a static point along the seashore and staring at it as hard as I could, yet still there were times I thought I might lose my lunch … and also my pride.

A few hours later, we pulled back into the harbor, and I thought to myself, "No more deep-sea fishing for me."

The truth is, the students we've reached through our PULSE events have felt the exact same way. *Anything* would be better than the chaos that had been throwing them up and down and this way and that.

They were waves tossed about on the whim of the wind, never knowing where they were headed or why. But then, enter Jesus, the Son of God. The rescue they'd felt was *tangible*. They'd found an anchor for the soul. I still get teary, thinking about their stories. They'd been *changed*. Because of Jesus, they'd been reset. And as they came to him with their longings for love and significance, for purpose and a "high," they realized that he alone could satisfy their needs.

Over time, this Jesus would prove to them that the more they trusted him, the more trustworthy they'd find him to be. He *really would* prove faithful. He *really would* provide for them. He *really would* protect them. He *really would* care. And so they would move forward, one baby step at a time, walking not by sight but by faith, following not their own path but his. They would quit defining themselves according to their Instagram likes in favor of affection from the Lover of their soul.

James 1 says,

> *If you don't know what you're doing,*
> *pray to the Father. He loves to help.*
> *You'll get his help, and won't be con-*
> *descended to when you ask for it. Ask*
> *boldly, believingly, without a second*
> *thought. People who "worry their*
> *prayers" are like wind-whipped waves.*
> *Don't think you're going to get anything*
> *from the Master that way, adrift at sea,*
> *keeping all your options open. (verses*
> *5–8, MSG)*

It's fitting language for what I've seen, time and time again, which is that as you close off all other options, choosing exclusively to tether yourself to Jesus, in return you get everything. Everything you've dreamed of and more.

AS YOU CLOSE OFF
ALL OTHER OPTIONS,
CHOOSING EXCLUSIVELY
TO TETHER YOURSELF
TO JESUS,
IN RETURN YOU GET
EVERYTHING.
EVERYTHING YOU'VE
DREAMED OF
AND MORE.

Which brings me to a straightforward question: Will you spend the sum of your life keeping your options open, or will you surrender yourself to Jesus? If you're holding this book in your hands and have gotten this far, I believe that God wants to offer you *significant* perspective, *significant* change, and *significant* hope. He's not angry with you. He's not fed up with you. He's not ashamed of you. He's not withholding his invitation of acceptance, grace, and love from you. Far from it. He is near to the brokenhearted and is wishing that no one should perish but that all (this includes you) would come into a saving relationship with him, through his Son, Jesus Christ. He loves you. He wants you. And he promises to perfect you once you come. Place your hope in him: his life, death, burial, and resurrection. Confess your mistakes and admit your need for him. Surrender and see *everything* change.

And so, come. Take the next step. Get to the church that is participating in the *Reset* series. Grab a Bible and bring it with you. Let God in. *Pray*—whether for the first time or the millionth. You will never regret what you do for God. You know what you'll regret? You'll regret what you *don't* do for him. If the most consequential thing that happens for you as a result of your reading this book and attending the *Reset* series is that you crack open a Bible, offer up a prayer or two to God, and set foot inside a local church for the first time in a long time, then I count that as a win. But secretly, here's what I suspect: God is up to something much, much bigger here. Take his plans for you seriously, and you'll discover what my buddies and I so desperately craved, back when we were curious, somewhat cynical would-be world changers: *life that is truly life*.

## About the Author

Nick Hall didn't set out to found PULSE, he set out to share the hope of Jesus on his college campus—and so many people's lives were impacted that PULSE was founded to help keep the message spreading.

As a voice to the next generation, Nick has shared the message of Jesus at hundreds of events to millions of students and is regularly featured as a speaker for pastors' gatherings, student conferences, training events, and festivals around the world. He has a passion for student-led prayer movements, leadership training, evangelism, and discipleship and has received hands-on training from some of the most influential Christian leaders of our day. He sits on the leadership teams for the US Lausanne Committee, the National Association of Evangelicals, and the student advisory team for the Billy Graham Evangelistic Association (BGEA) and is a partner evangelist with the Luis Palau Association. In the spring of 2011, he was welcomed to the National Facilitation Committee for the Mission America Coalition (MAC). Nick has a bachelor's degree in Business Administration from North Dakota State University and a master's in Leadership and Christian Thought from Bethel Seminary in St. Paul, Minnesota. Nick and his wife, Tiffany, have two children and live in Minneapolis, Minnesota.